MW01206537

Copyright © 2025

The Hoserrific Corporation

joelcjoelc@gmail.com

Tennis Tips

That Could Also Be

Sex Therapy

For your partner. Or partner.

By Dr. Wendy J.

A good sex therapist and a
mediocre tennis player.

Don't be intimidated. Sure, most people started as teenagers but if you didn't, with effort, you can be as good as they are. Maybe better.

Communication is key. Talk with your partner before, after and during.

Balls have a lifespan. When the fuzz is gone and they don't bounce like they used to, consider replacing them.

It's okay if after, you just had a good sweat. You don't always need a "victory"

The Eastern grip is a good place to start for beginners.

When thinking about the head, consider your height and weight. If it's not right, it can cause pain in your wrist or elbow.

Make sure to follow through, no matter what motion you're using.

Timing is key. You don't want to be too early or too late. Many beginners find they are way too early.

Start every stroke in a ready position with your hips parallel.

Keep your contact point in front of you with your non-dominant hand.

When you're well-balanced, on time, and your contact point is right, you will feel the satisfaction of hitting the sweet spot.

As you're learning, keep things simple. Focus on just returning whatever comes your way.

Remember, it's supposed to be fun. Don't get mad if you miss sometimes.

Always try to keep your head still.

Don't move too much. Only move when you see a shot is coming.

Getting your back leg and weight behind a ball allows for easier weight transfer and more consistency.

Focus on accuracy versus force.

Practice on your own. In your backyard, basement, or even on your driveway.

Move yourself into a position where you feel comfortable. From there you will be able to generate more power.

To really get better, you need to play with several different partners.

If it's not going where you want,
maybe look at your grip.

If you hear a loud "twang", look down – you may have broken something.

Try a stabilizer. It's a small plastic disc that wedges into the head and keeps the vibrations down.

Know where you are at all times.
Avoid finding yourself in "no man's
land."

If your partner calls it "out," even if you think it's in, just accept it and try again.

Visualize making solid contact.

It is extremely helpful to watch videos of other people doing it.

Many women, and even men, find grunting helps as they release power.

If people are watching, tune them out. Focus on what <u>you</u> are doing.

Don't be afraid to try new equipment.

Spinning is helpful, but only if you can control things and keep it in.

If the surface is too wet, try later when things dry off.

Your ball toss should go straight up and come straight down about 18 inches in front of your leading foot.

Repetition leads to improvement. You can ever rent a machine to help you.

Consider going to one of those camps in Florida where pros watch you, coach you, and even join you.

Avoid comparing your partner to past partners. No one likes being compared.

Know your limitations. Decide how much time, energy, and resources you're able to devote to yourself and your partner.

Breathe! Breathing exercises
will reduce anxiety and increase
relaxation, promoting a deeper
connection with one's body and
partner.

Don't aim for the same spot every time. Explore!

If things aren't consistently working out how you planned, it may be time for a medical check-up.

If it feels out of control, don't be afraid to slow it down.

Before you start swinging, make
sure you know what your goal is.

When starting, know which box you are aiming for.

Stay agile. Standing close means balls will reach you faster, so stay on your toes and show no fear.

Master the fundamental strokes before moving on to more complex ones.

Fuel up! Eat at least an hour before and again right after to make sure you have enough energy to finish.

Hydrate!   Drink before and again during breaks or changeovers.

Focus on your footwork. Ladder
drills and cone exercises can help.

Film your sessions. In the thick of it, it can be hard to note your mistakes. Reviewing a video will show you the truth.

Don't neglect the mental aspect. Success comes as much from your brain as your body.

Depth matters. Get it deep to stop your opponent from rushing forward.

Aim for full extension as you make contact.

Try partners of different ages. You may be surprised by what you can learn from older partners with years of experience.

Don't let formal instruction keep you from getting started and having fun.

Stay patient as you learn. Remember that it takes time to get the hang of it.

Prevent injuries with proper warm up and cool down.   Stretching is important as is core, back, and shoulder exercises.

You can still do it with three people. You just need to establish rules before and be open to a slightly different experience.

Rest is important. Sleep leads to better stamina.

For fun, try it on different surfaces – clay, grass, etc.

Sure, you could have a family member as your partner, but it's really better not to – it introduces a lot of outside emotions and may make both partners uncomfortable.

Made in the USA
Columbia, SC
24 June 2025